A YOUNG GIRL READING
Jean-Honoré Fragonard
National Gallery of Art, Washington, D.C.
Gift of Mrs. Mellon Bruce
in memory of her father, Andrew W. Mellon

Willa Brown

Legacy

THE PROVIDENCE OF GOD
IS MY INHERITANCE

Legacy

by

Eric Sloane

A Funk & Wagnalls Book
Published by Thomas Y. Crowell
New York

I dedicate to those who lend an ear
To find a thought in what they hear:
And pray that I may teach some other eyes to see
The visions which my God has given me.

Designer: Stephanie Winkler

Library of Congress Cataloging in Publication Data

Sloane, Eric.
  Legacy.
  "A Funk and Wagnalls book."
  1. Sloane, Eric.   2. United States—Biography.
3. United States—Civilization. I. Title.
CT275.S52352A33   741'.092'4 [B]   78-22455
ISBN 0-308-10351-3

79 80 81 82 83 10 9 8 7 6 5 4 3 2

Contents

Foreword

An author receives all sorts of mail, some critical, some in praise. I'm grateful for both. Two letters arrived at once recently, that seemed to have a supernatural relationship. I believe there is someone up there who gives quick and miraculous advice, easily recognizable if only you are alert.

"Dear Mr. Sloane," started the first letter (from my publisher). "What about a new book?"

When you get to be my age, new ideas become less frequent. You find yourself telling the same jokes over and over. If you are an author, you will find yourself writing books that you have already written many years ago. I felt certain what my reply to the publisher would be.

The second letter was a startler because it nicely replied to the first. From a Mrs. Waldemar Szmanski, it said: "Dear Mr. Sloane. I have admired your work for many years. On July 4th I gave birth to a beautiful baby boy and now I am proud and honored to inform you that I have named him Eric Sloane Szmanski. I hope your namesake will show in his life the talent you have shown in yours, and so I would be grateful if you might write to this child, giving advice as to how a young man should conduct himself in order to have a meaningful and rewarding life. I shall save your words for his twenty-first birthday."

Whoever is up there, thank you! That unusual letter gave me the idea for this book. Who knows but Eric Sloane Szmanski might someday become a painter and writer. Or even a thinker.

One day on Long Island when I found myself traveling through the area of Brookville, where I had lived many years ago, I decided to see if the little saltbox house I had once built was still there. I remembered how hard it was for me to hand-hew the beams, how I had worked to create an antique mood, then how the people who bought my place painted over the beams and plastered over the ancient panels, covering most of my efforts.

The house has been resold several times since then, but I was pleased to find that the present owner had now scraped down the beams to their original patina, brought back to life the old panels, even uncovered my original fireplace construction. "I found your big mantel beam," he told me, "with an inscription carved into it—'The providence of God is my inheritance.' Did *you* carve that wording into the beam, and what is the story behind it?"

Indeed I was the one who had carved it, and I have done the same in every house I have built since. But there was something profound about that original carved thought having been covered over for so many years, then coming to light now with even more meaning than ever. It brought back a thousand memories and I was pleased to recall the story.

As a young man, I had squandered all that was left to me by my father: that financial suicide now seemed ruinous, leaving me in a morose and distressed frame of mind. It was not only a personal mistake but a grievous insult to my parents, bordering on ingratitude. Either with self-punishment in mind, or as an escape from reality, I set off to nowhere with a pack on my back as an itinerant sign painter. I suppose I was like what we refer to now as flower children or hippies, yet I did have a crew haircut, I did keep my white overalls tidy, and I did diligently work my way across the nation. It gave me time to think and to salve my conscience.

If it hadn't been for a sudden shower one Sunday in the Mid-

Coming in out of the rain

west, and my having to get in out of the rain, I would never have sought a church, but the countryside was drenched; I was grateful for the shelter. The service was under way. I took off my pack and settled into a back pew, feeling very wet and a bit out of place. Being in a church carried me back to childhood memories and I also pondered my present condition, not really listening at all to the preacher's sermon. Then for some unexplainable reason he seemed to fix his gaze upon me. It was almost as if he had singled me out from the rest of the congregation. "The providence of God," he thundered, quoting from his biblical notes, "is your *inheritance!*" As if struck, I returned to consciousness.

Until that instant I had regarded the word *providence* as a synonym for paradise; of course, it is also the name of a city in Rhode Island, but suddenly I realized that providence really meant *"provide-*ance" and at once knew that I still owned the greatest inheritance of all, one that I could never dissipate: I would always be *provided* for! It was a new and encouraging thought for me to live by.

Now some threescore and ten years later I am aware of divine providence and I have become all the more convinced that the most valuable fortune anyone can amass during a lifetime is not material wealth but the things he *learns;* his beliefs and convictions rather than his possessions can be the richest inheritance. The price of wisdom is indeed far above that of rubies.

Therefore, being of sound mind, I have now disposed of the major part of my earthly possessions, so there is comparatively little in material property left to bequeath to those I leave behind. Having lived a thoughtful life with the hope that it might not have all been in vain, it now seems a proper time for me to gather in print my beliefs and convictions so that I may pass them on to whoever might accept them. Thoreau said that to inherit material property is not to be born at all but to be still-born. To inherit knowledge, however, is to receive the riches of life. Fortunately, too, there is no inheritance tax on wisdom!

Knowledge exists to be imparted, but unasked-for advice is rude and seldom listened to, so I hope my words are not misinterpreted as unprovoked advice. There are those who prefer to learn everything by themselves, by experience or by what is known as "the hard way," but in spite of its heralded merits, the hard-way method happens to be the hard way. Experience operates the most expensive school. Then, too, there are those who spend their whole lives in the rugged schools of experience without ever graduating and making use of what they have learned. I suppose it is sometimes unfortunate that we have the right to do what we want with our own lives.

I remember, at the age of fifty-nine, marrying a girl of eighteen (she was very pretty). One of the first things she wanted to do was to paint our kitchen a color in vogue at that time called shocking pink. I explained that I had done that very thing long before she was born, and it just didn't work. "That may be so," she complained, "but I *do* want to paint it that color just to see for *myself* how it turns out. If I don't like it, I promise to change it. I want to learn things for myself." She had a perfect right to learn by experience, but on her own time, not mine. That marriage was a short one. I am sure she has since had her shocking-pink kitchen and in time has changed it.

The anecdotes of life can be funny or profound, yet they are a continuous spectacle of predicaments that should not be forgotten and never considered meaningless. Down to the tiniest biochemical process of nature I believe there is nothing meaningless in life: I believe there is nothing in all creation without value.

So whether accepted as serious food for thought, as just pleasant autobiographical meanderings, or as one person's legacy to another, this book allows me to feel better for having declared this will and, with your permission, filed it in the safe deposit of your mind.

Eric Sloane
Warren, Connecticut

*built for
tomorrow*

The Adventure of Being Aware

Once upon a time as I sat in the manger of an abandoned Bucks County barn, I tried to decipher the scrawled inscription on a foundation stone. The Pennsylvania Germans were known for inscribing names and dates and familiar maxims, probably because they lived in so meaningful an era and because they were so aware of that. This inscription, however, was not done as an exterior architectural decoration but was made on the inside of the barn as if it had been done as a reminder to the farmer himself. *We are here*, it read, *for a reason.*

It is strange how a simple thought like that can awaken you with explosive force, implying that individual thinking could be merely a fragment of universal mind. Maxims are little sermons designed to be remembered along the path of life, and this one has had the power to stay with me. In an age full of people without purpose, I was fortunate to be guided by two purposeful inspirations: *The providence of God is my inheritance,* and *I am here for a reason.*

I am grateful that these thoughts have made me aware and appreciative of my existence. Indeed a pertinent lesson of life is that we cannot take existence for granted.

It was an ancient belief that each lifetime be reserved for the dedication to the study of some particular knowledge, such as the concept of *truth* or *gratitude* or *teaching* or *suffering* or any of the many spiritual standards of human life. That belief, of course, involves the reincarnation of spirit so that after many lives and many accumulations of knowledge there could finally emerge among us an omnipotent mentality, a divine manifestation of the Creator such as a Christ. This idea, of course, suggests that every one of us might now be in that very process and that our present life could (or could not, as we see fit) be an important step toward the final perfection of an exalted being.

Youth is not the only time for such philosophical daydreaming and we all at some time or another contemplate the possibility of reincarnation; so I have often wondered if whatever I am learning now might be carried on into some future existence. I have even been on the lookout for some lesson pertinent to my present-day living that might enhance a future mentality.

If asked to name the most valuable endowment that my adventures have taught me so far, I think I might choose the lesson of *awareness*. This is a peculiar gift that the artist *inherits*, seldom a learnable subject.

I first discovered awareness while trying to pinpoint the difference between the Americans of yesterday and the Americans of today. My conclusion was that we now seem to have lost the fine art of being awake. We have deteriorated to the present condition of living in a psychedelic, mechanical dreamworld of apathy, living in a lackadaisical and dangerous degree of unawareness.

Awareness might be defined as the state of being awake. Of course, we all presume to be fully awake, yet we actually exist in a partial state of mental and spiritual sleep. Even as you read these words (and even as I wrote them) we were both influenced by a certain degree of sleep. It is almost impossible to comprehend that sleeping and waking could be similar kinds of consciousness and that we practice them only in different degrees of intensity. To be completely asleep, however, we would have to be near death (in unconsciousness) and to be completely awake (for even a short while) would be strenuous enough to render the average person stricken weak and unbelievably tired from so profound an experience.

I have often heard how during some extraordinary threat of disaster, or in an instant of intense fright, a person's "whole life passed before him." That, I believe, is a phenomenon of complete wakefulness, where in a flashing second we become aware of everything, including our whole life. In that frightful instant we were completely awake.

I have often wondered why instances of childhood remain so vivid, why although I cannot recall what I ate or where I dined only a day or two ago, I do recall certain unimportant feelings or sights or sounds that occurred sixty years ago. Now I realize it was because my alert, receptive child's mind was startled into even more wakefulness than is possible now in my dulled and aged consciousness.

Of course, there are exceptions to our natural unawareness; I do recall exactly where I was and what I was doing at the instant of the blackout in New York; I recall the same when I heard the news of Pearl Harbor, and I can also relive the instant when I heard of President Kennedy's assassination. These small shocks simply caused me to be more awake and so they left more indelible impressions.

My researches revealed that the early American was privileged to live in a remarkably constant state of awareness. The endless parade of epidemics, emergencies, threats of Indians, weather— all the elements of fear that surrounded pioneer life—kept him always alert and awake. Furthermore, everything the agrarian pioneer touched or wore or ate or drank or devised was an original product of his own labor. He was aware of how his drinking water differed from that of his neighbor; he grew his own food; he cut his own fuel and made his own light. His was an existence of his own design, a world of constant awareness, producing a satisfying joy impossible nowadays when we take existence for granted.

Each day as we become more mechanized, we become less awake, less aware, always more under the influence of external powers beyond our comprehension. Electricity, TV, radio, machines or even the simple clock is beyond what the average mind completely understands (or really wishes to understand). The ballet of city life is a performance of half-awake mechanical people who do not have to exercise a mentality of their own. No one is doing things by or for themselves and we just go through puppetlike motions, waiting for things to happen. We are becoming machines.

A machine does not have to think or remember, therefore it

has no conscience. Although we feign conscience and feebly mouth it, we are usually too far into sleep consciousness to wake up and fully declare it. Theoretically, if two opposing armies were suddenly to become completely awake, the war would cease. By the same token, the more military matériel and information we collect, the more we are expected to make use of it and so there is yet more consciousness to make war. The fact that the world now spends about a million dollars each minute for military purposes is evidence that man is existing in an illogical dreamworld, allowing others to do the thinking and to make decisions for him. Apathy itself is a living oblivion.

There is no doubt about it, we are all here for a reason, but when we are lulled into that unawareness of partial sleep, we forget what the reason is. Indifference or apathy can become a devastating disease; when it becomes a national characteristic, it foretells disaster. It is impossible to be sleepy and courageous at the same time, and the decline in American courage has already become a dangerous symptom of national unconsciousness. It was strange that it took a Russian to cry out "America awake!" but Alexander Solzhenitsyn warned us of what is happening to a sleepy unaware America, as we lose the moral stamina to defend our freedom.

We live in a constant dreamworld of indecision, even down to what we eat and drink. "What will you have?" we say to our dinner partner at the restaurant. "I don't know," he will reply, "what are *you* having?" Ask any question nowadays and you will usually get another question as a reply. "What shall we do tomorrow?" will bring "I don't know—what would *you* like to do?" The least thing a weak personality wants to do is to decide. It doesn't take much strength to do things, but deciding what to do is the greatest problem we have today.

A gift to be cherished, life was planned by the Creator to be a joyous experience of awareness and it used to be just that. Now when we turn on a faucet without knowing where the water comes from (and don't care), there is a certain loss of interest and satisfaction. When we switch on a light, we don't know where the power originated and couldn't be less concerned. After one blackout, the power utilities tried to find out where the power had originated and they still don't know for certain.

A candle might give less light than electricity, but if it came from wax made in your own kitchen, by wicks spun from your own flax, and dipped by your own mother, the light would suddenly become more meaningful, even precious. If you spun wool from your own sheep to make your own clothing, even a pair of socks would become valuable works of art and a special joy to wear.

We are amazed nowadays at "how the old-timers used to save things," with attics full of clothing and household items; the truth is that they were not as frugal as they were *aware*. The value of those saved things was the rich awareness of who had *made* them or who had *worn* them. Sentiment itself is awareness.

Nowadays we aren't sure if our clothing was made in Newark or Tokyo and so its worth to us involves only money value. All that is left for us now is a dehumanized life in which the sole part we play is to pay money for the various privileges of existence.

If you wish to experience a strange joy, an interruption of your sleep consciousness, a startling feeling of content, and a simple relaxation that you will long remember, go somewhere in the country and take a deep breath; then let out the darndest yell! Believe it or not, it will take a lot of courage to do; you will even risk embarrassment to your own sleeping self because you will be doing something you were not expected to do. I tried it and found myself unduly concerned that someone might hear me and become alarmed, so I changed my loud yell into a loud song (how frightened we are of what others may think!). Don't try this trick in the city among the other unawake people or you will probably get yourself arrested. There really isn't a law against letting out a yell, but you will be accused of "disturbing the peace." (*Peace in a big city?*)

The emotion of being aware is an extraordinary, exhilarating adventure, but the first step to this experience is self-awareness. To yourself, you are the most important being in the whole world. To the Creator, you are also important, for He put you here for a reason and He expects you to *become aware of the reason*.

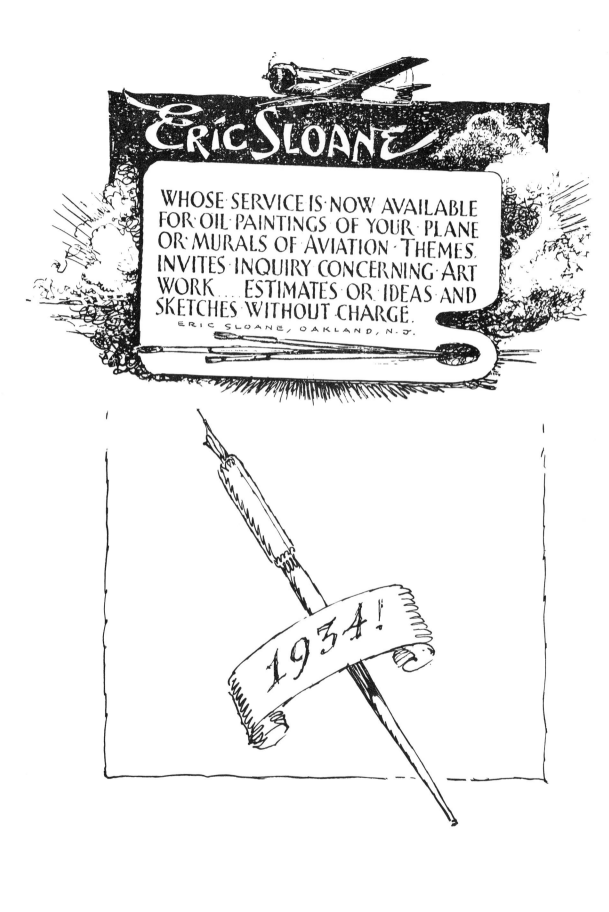

The Adventure of Painting

Adventure is not outside us but within. Everything in life can be an adventure. Each tiny act, each thought, even each stroke of a painter's brush can be full of suspense and excitement. The artist's life, incidentally, is particularly rich with adventure, for each painting is a completely new enterprise.

A painter usually cringes when confronted with early examples of his own work. It is like meeting an ex-wife. The sketch shown on the opposite page, however, brought me only good memories; it also brought the realization of how little we manage to change during the long years. Forty-five years ago, when I had first decided to make painting the sky my life's work, I did this black and white announcement in a 1934 newspaper. I am amazed that the airplane I dreamed up then is remarkably modern in design and that my lettering was done in quite the same style as I would do now.

At that time I had yet to do an "aviation mural" but recently I completed a cloud painting in Washington, D.C., that was possibly conceived those many years ago. Stressing in the advertisement that "estimates or ideas and sketches are without charge" hints that I might have been a bit hungry at the time, yet I still go along with that offer, so I suppose I shall never change. Art is long and time is fleeting, but that old advertisement reminds me that every painter was first an amateur. A good dream never dies.

19

Bill Lear, who designed airplane radios then and later invented the Learjet, had his factory at Roosevelt Field, Long Island, where he let me have studio space. Instead of paying Bill rent, I contracted to do a block-long sign on the roof. I'd never made a sign that big, and I used an ordinary house broom as a brush.

Bill, who had a great sense of humor, told his flying friends that having Eric Sloane paint license numbers or lettering on their planes was an omen of good luck, and fliers in those days were a superstitious lot. One round-the-world flier named De Pinedo scoffed at the superstition after I offered to do some lettering on his Bellanca airplane which later crashed as it tried to leave Floyd Bennett Field. From then on, trans-ocean and race pilots went out of their way for a Sloane sign job. It kept me in pocket money.

I offered to paint pictures of people's airplanes because I presumed that those who had enough money to own their own planes might also have enough to buy paintings of them. Most owners, I soon learned, however, had little money left after buying their airplanes. But I did know that art should be a way of life instead of a business and that aviation pictures were not really art; so my airplanes kept getting smaller while the clouds kept getting bigger. Finally I ventured to paint that which I loved most—just the vast expanse of sky, and I coined the word *cloudscape*.

Some asked when I intended "to add the plane," and others said, "What's *that* supposed to be—*just sky?*" At least (I reasoned) I'd be the only idiot in the world to paint such an unsalable subject as mere clouds, and since that made me a specialist, I could ask outrageous prices for my work. Then someone named Amelia Earhart bought one of my airplane-less cloudscapes. That cinched my plans, ending my career of being an airplane painter, and I began at once to work toward the justification of a career as the American sky artist.

However, my business with the sky was interrupted one day when I stood in the penetrating loneliness of an abandoned New England barn and felt the presence of the great American past. Just as a sudden accident can end a man's career, an instant mood can change the path of a well-chosen pursuit. It was a lifetime ago, but I recall that instant clearly, standing in the barn on hay that was strewn there over a century earlier but still perfumed the stillness. I remember how that quiet was broken by the faraway drone of an airplane, like background music to the contrast of yesterday and today. Perhaps that old barn was waiting for it to happen, because the communication was magic; I was confronted with an overwhelming call and I decided that painting the sky could wait. It was an interruption that lasted for half a century.

Now, three dozen books later, and a few thousand rural Americana paintings, I am sometimes melancholy about the results, for instead of relating that poignant instant in the ancient barn and recapturing the meaningful glory of early American society, I might have only contributed to just so much senseless nostalgic "Americana." I wasn't trying to paint *buildings,* I had been trying to paint the American *spirit!*

The very words you are now reading were interrupted by a telephone call. I suppose it could have been a metaphysical response to my writing and thinking of the moment, but it was from a manufacturer asking if his firm could use my paintings to advertise his "Americana products." His voice was inspiring and enthusiastic, but his theme was dismal to me. "What we want to do," he said, "is to remind people of the American heritage. Your old barns and covered bridges and ancient tools and log cabins tell the story best." Of course, I had failed miserably, for the American heritage is none of these things. In fact, the American heritage isn't any *thing* or *things;* it is a *spirit.*

The early American had magnificent spirit and profound purpose. He created his homestead for future generations with sincere preparation for them to be independent people. He lived in an agrarian age of self-dependence and barter; money had not yet become the foundation of our national economy. Every American's trust was in God. The American knew his reason for being and he had that rare awareness of his past, his present, and his future. All this seemed a gospel worthy of any painter's labor and *this* is what I have been trying to preach in oils all these years.

One kindly newspaper commentator recently remarked that "when Sloane dies there need be no name on his gravestone—just *here lies an interpreter of Americana.*" Little did he

.... the Sky could wait.

know that I already considered such a nameless marker but with the simpler epitaph: *God knows I tried.*

Without pointing a finger, shaking a fist or bitterly lamenting the loss of traditional values, I have spent more than fifty years depicting the beauty of our early farm life, painting the national landscape, and illustrating the original American way of living. Splendid as a painting may be, however, if it is a painting without noble purpose, in my mind it is only decoration and might as well not have been done. And so I hope I have not spent these many years merely presenting decorative paintings and writing entertaining Americana pieces instead of "painting with a pen and writing with a brush" about the vanished *values* of America past. I sometimes shudder at seeing my calendar art contributions, which seem to please those who consider art the beauty parlor of civilization, and I spend restless nights wondering if I have just supplied material for nostalgia.

A painter should never be completely satisfied with himself or his work, so I shall try to be content and continue being a student. When I look at the masters' works, I am brought to tears by their greatness and I am spurred on, always trying to become an artist. That word "artist" is used loosely nowadays; I always believed (as with the word *"genius"*) that it is presumptuous for anyone to call himself an *artist*. The early American used such titles as limner, portrait and landscape painter, illustrator, muralist, and so on, but now anyone who can brave the inside of a fashionable gallery by expressing himself indiscriminately on a flat surface seems to automatically earn the title of *artist*.

The artist is one who without effort inhabits a higher sphere of thought into which others rise with some difficulty and labor. It is not for me to say that I inhabit such an exalted plane, but I am flattered beyond imagination and grateful to those few who think I do. Meanwhile, I enjoy the comfort of calling myself just a *painter*.

"Talent" is another loosely used word among painters and critics. What you mostly see at the art galleries is not talent but "ability." That indescribable something you sometimes *feel* is the genius of that one talented painter in a thousand.

The exaltation of "talent," as it is called, is a curse of our time. Talent and ability are usually regarded as one and the same thing, but they are really far apart, sometimes even opposites. The art of drawing or taking paint from a tube and depositing it prettily and convincingly on canvas is a craft, yet craftsmanship is not talent. Craft can be taught but there are no teachers of talent.

I suppose during the years I have received hundreds of inquiries about what one should do for the "gifted child." According to my belief, the proper answer is *nothing*. Real talent (genius) will express itself whether encouraged or discouraged; with too much notice, however, it may become confused and stifled. Aside from the miracle of birth, witnessing your own child draw that first image is a most profound revelation. Even first attempts at speech cannot compare with the first expressions of communication with crayon and paper: The proud parent is usually convinced that he is witnessing extraordinary newborn talent.

Talent is not the art of doing as much as it is the art of *seeing*, of *feeling*, and of *knowing*, long before any work at all is done. The painter-artist, then, must first excel in seeing and feeling and knowing, long before he contemplates the craft of actually doing. The true artist is a *see-er*, gifted with the ability of seeing that which others look at but fail to see, and the painter-artist's reason for being is to reveal to those who have looked without seeing, *exactly what they have missed*. The artist extends this valuable gift of awareness; in so doing, he enriches the life of others.

The decorator who makes pleasing or fashionable designs that delight the eye but offer little or nothing to stimulate the mind is not as much a communicator as an *entertainer*. Along with the average person, I regard the Jackson Pollock type of painting (great as it may be) more entertaining than communicative. Designs (like any other entertainment to the senses) become boring in time.

A bore is a communicative person with nothing to communicate; the decorative painter with nothing to communicate runs that sort of risk. An *imparting* painting is never boring because it changes constantly with the moods of the beholder and leaves a spiritual stimulation.

As I walked down my lane to my mailbox one day I was surprised by all the wonders of growing things along the way that I had missed during my usual hasty trips by automobile. Halfway

down the lane I came upon a patch of long-stemmed autumn blossoms that danced a yard above the ground from slender, almost invisible black stems. The result was like a thousand stars floating in space, all reflecting back the radiance of the morning sun. Although collecting my mail had shortly before been important to me, I suddenly had an uncontrollable urge to hasten back to the studio for camera or pencil to capture the sight and a half hour later there was a finished recollection in color on my easel. It was not until the work was done that I remembered about my mail and then I wondered why I had acted so irrationally.

Why, when we witness some remarkable thing, is there that uncontrollable urge to share the experience with someone else? The answer came quickly when my wife, Mimi, came to my studio and glanced at my painting. "Oh, you've done those weeds along the driveway! I guess I didn't realize how beautiful they were until now!" I knew at once that the artist is simply an expert at cherishing consciousness, and that his reason for being is to record that consciousness so that others may experience it. It is important to know one's reason for being and it is satisfying to be aware of why we work.

I believe that art schools do not actually teach *art*, but there, instead, a student learns artistic *crafts*. I am convinced, however, that the most important learning for anyone who wants to be an artist is not *how* to work but *why;* this should be a most important learning in any school. After realizing *why* we work, learning becomes easier and it can often be accomplished without any instruction at all. By my way of thinking, most art teachers are really teachers of craft, but the true teacher of art *shows a student how to learn art for himself.*

If one wishes to become a true artist, technical knowledge is not enough; the artist transcends technique so that his communication is the result of the unconscious rather than a graphic exchange. The art of attuning to the unconscious (an ability that the artist usually *inherits*) could be more a spiritual study through Zen than anything learned in an art school.

In the old days when student painters learned "under a master," the teacher didn't give instruction but instead allowed his apprentices to watch him at work and therefore to think for themselves. The best advice I ever received in an art school was when I asked my teacher to criticize my drawing. "If you yourself can't see what is right and what is wrong with your work," he said, "then you really shouldn't be drawing." I thought him rude and insulting at the time but now I know what he meant and I am thankful for what he said. He gave me the gift of confidence in myself and that is the most important lesson of all.

Having never kept a scrapbook, and having made a habit of trying to forget each painting as soon as I've finished with it, I still believe that art students might do well to destroy their early works at once instead of collecting them. They may be fairly good work, but then there's nothing more dull than fairly good violin playing. Only the very *best* is worthy of collecting, except as a curiosity. Hardly a month goes by now but some stranger seeks me out for a visit who "just happens to have" with him a scrapbook of his old art-school drawings, asking if I will look at them. "Sorry," I always say, "but everything I look at influences my own work, so I'd rather not venture to see anyone else's. You didn't just happen to have the drawings with you anyway! I'll bet you've been carrying them around with you for years, falling in love with them. My advice, if that's what you really want, is to throw them all away." I don't make many friends that way, but the chronic advice seeker is a sorry soul who needs shock more than he needs advice.

Destroying your own work is nothing new in the world of art: I have seen many an old master's painting with another (discarded) painting on the back of the canvas, and many works of the great have been done directly on top of a washed-out subject. After working on a tiresome painting for weeks, it takes courage to smear it beyond finishing, but that brave smear can be a stroke of genius. I have destroyed a dozen uninspired tries only to end with a fresh and satisfactory piece of work. The confession of poor work is the beginning of something better.

After working for a day or two on one large black and white drawing, I found a smudge of ink that could not be properly hidden or corrected, and so I contemplated what to do about it. "What's the problem?" asked my studio cleaning lady, who always senses my predicaments. "It's that smudge," I said. "I'm considering chucking the drawing and starting out again from scratch." That, to her, called for a suggestion. "I'd just leave it that way," she said, "and sell it at a discount." As proper comment to that, I emptied my whole inkwell on the work. God replies in strange ways.

Knowing when to condemn your own work is an occasional art;

a more important and constant knowledge is simply knowing when to stop. Not knowing when to stop is a frequent human failing: I have a thousand times made an oil sketch of merit and then painted away all its good qualities with tedious craftsmanship. It happens with authors and politicians and lecturers, even with lovers; few of us know enough to stop while we are ahead. Art directors will agree that the preliminary rough sketch very often has more artistic merit and more of the artist than his final finished work.

Taking too much time to produce a work can also become a bad habit. For some strange reason, art is often valued by the time it takes to do it; even the painter falls into that trap. I once labored for hours and days at making each and every blade of grass in a field until I learned the finer art of giving the same impression with just one smashing stroke of a nearly dry brush. Just as your signature is at its best when written at a fairly fast pace, a labored signature would lose character: a tediously done piece of art work is never a good example of your artistic individuality. A curse on those whose constant habit is to ask painters, "How long did it take to do?" That to me is too personal (and very rude), and the question doesn't deserve a reply.

There is constant mention nowadays of *creative art* and *creative artists*, something that seems to have evolved in the twentieth century. Before then, I do believe, there was only one creative artist and all creative art consisted of His works. Obviously, there is now either a misuse of the word "creative," a misrepresentation among modern artists, or perhaps there are a lot of Jehovahs exhibiting in the fashionable galleries.

God creates and man strives to *re-create*. My joy in writing or painting is experienced when I have re-created and brought to life some past consciousness, some profound instant, or some stirring sight that once aroused my emotion. I believe that art is the portrayal of remembrances, that even the greatest artist is not creative but completely *re*-creative. Those who claim that they are creative are deceiving both themselves and the public.

Sometimes as I work, a slip of the brush or what I call a "happy accident" will create an effect far beyond my actual capability as a painter. Perhaps it will give an effect of sunlight on old barnwood, such as I witnessed one time (maybe it was last week or last year or during some poignant instant when I was a little boy). That bygone instant rekindled by the slip of my brush might then change the subject of my painting and inspire me to work the whole picture around that tiny, happy accident.

Now the scene changes to a man walking along the avenue with no thought of buying art. He suddenly stops at a gallery window to look at that painting. He, too, as a little boy, had experienced such an instant as I portrayed in my painting and it now brings back that precious memory to him. He thinks he is buying art when he purchases my painting, but he is really buying back an instant of his own life: I had painted my own memory and he bought his own memory.

This method of painting by happy accidents is anything but disciplined; my easel and painting paraphernalia attest to that. When I open a tube of paint I have yet to replace the top. I do finger painting with my oils and I have learned now to paint using work gloves to minimize the effects of lead poison. I have probably used a ton of rags and my friends give me rags for both Christmas and birthdays. I was about to describe my eccentric method of painting as being the work of a slob, but decided to first look up that inelegant word in my *American Heritage Dictionary;* there I found the word "slob" preceded by the name John Sloan, accompanied by a photograph of my old teacher doing a painting. Instead of a hand palette, John Sloan mixed his paints on a flat slab of Masonite, a practice of my own, which affords me constant Masonite kindling for my fireplace. Now and then a friend will retrieve one of my castaways and ask me to sign it. I wonder if these sloppy originals might become just as important as a finished oil painting, for a used palette embodies much of the painter's color thoughts and free expression.

Art is the reflection of its time and so modern art happens to be a true mirror of modern times. On the walls of any "modern museum" you will see all the variations of escape from that conglomeration of mad uncertainty known as today: You will sense the hostility toward tradition and the absence of purpose that prevails in today's life. You will also see American sculpture welded from cast-off junk, such as a discarded bicycle wheel and even a men's urinal, all hailed as works of art.

"Untitled, mixed media" is accepted as a suitable explanation for many modern works of art, but the artist's mind, too, is likely to be "mixed and without identity." I cannot imagine a man not worthy of a name, or a book without a title; but perhaps I can understand why some of those "modern" paintings are untitled!

In my time, people used to get their wit in jokebooks; there was one great American humor magazine called *Judge*. These are all gone from today's scene, but if you really need a laugh, just look at the titles of the works of art in modern galleries and museums. One of my favorites (featured in *Arts Magazine*, October 1975) is a discarded railroad tie resting in the middle of the gallery floor. It is identified as "Untitled, wood and creosote, 8"x8"x9'." I can just see the fashionable critics oohing and aahing over that one. There is also a heap of old rags thrown on the floor of one gallery titled "Rags, 60 inches by 62 inches." In another California gallery there was a creation (obviously of the artist's dog) "Untitled, mixed excrement media, 8 inches x 8 inches." I do enjoy the story of one exhibit consisting of a number of bricks arranged to make an interesting composition. The arrangement was sold to an overseas museum, but the bricks, of course, had to be dismantled and shipped in a box. Part of the deal was that the "sculptor" had to fly overseas and arrange the bricks back into their original position. Who needs a jokebook?

Recently my friend Don Kendall, who heads Pepsico, was asked by Yale University to speak on the subject of his corporate art collection. Don, who wanted to be accompanied by two working artists, sent to London for the sculptor David Wynn and I flew in from Santa Fe. Don, David and I met at New Haven, compared our speeches and proceeded to Yale's Hall of Sculpture where the lecture was to be presented. Yale University, however, seemed to have forgotten the occasion and there was no one on hand but the dean, who had never heard of us (or even the proposed lecture). "Sorry about that," he said, "but while you are here, you might as well see some of the students' work." He unlocked an all-white room that looked like an empty tennis court embellished in the center with what appeared to be a large brick and a triangle of beams. "How do you like it?" he said. "This is conceptual sculpture." He then proceeded to the next exhibit, a similar white room but with a black matlike rectangle painted in the center of the floor. "Another masterpiece of conceptual sculpture," he said proudly. "But I thought sculpture had to be three dimensional," I timidly ventured. He looked at me scornfully. "There *is* a third dimension here," he said, waving his arms overhead as if he were trying to part invisible curtains, "but *you* evidently are not capable of seeing it!"

I attended Yale art school before that dean was born, and I have given the best of my life and efforts to what I thought was art. I remember when painting was painting and sculpture was sculpture and I liked it best that way.

The Davenport, Iowa, Mid-Mississippi Art Competition recently gave a large cash award to the winning exhibit, described as "fibre wall-hanging in off-white with a range of interesting textures and central phallic shape." The object proved later to be an old mitten chewed into shreds by the winner of that art prize, a six-year-old Afghan hound.

My latest (and perhaps last) modern-museum visit included a viewing in a downstairs hall inscribed "men's room." I found a waiting line there and one gentleman told me that there was no room inside. I went ahead of the line, however, and cautiously opened the door. "I don't really have to *go*," I explained. "I merely want to *look*." I found it interesting, significant, and gratifying that the installed plumbing works of art were completely traditional and functional, and so I left knowing that at least one exhibit in the museum was completely sane and that there is still hope in the world of modern art.

Emerson said that the inventor knows how to borrow intelligently and that every man is (or should be) an inventor, but that was before painters specialized in invention. Someone said that a genius is one who does something that nobody ever did before, so now those painters and sculptors who imagine themselves geniuses depend largely upon uniqueness. The result is that most modern galleries display inventions rather than works of art, and there you will find the stupidest and most useless inventions in all the world. I'm all for inventing, but inventing for the sake of inventing has a certain madness about it, with works that seem to end up in either asylums or modern-art museums.

Cleverness is useful in everything but sufficient for nothing. After viewing the clever inventions that dominate most modern galleries, you will in time begin to reason that no matter what importance is granted to it, great art is rarely clever and, in the long run, clever art is seldom great. Clever people are good, but they are never best: clever people often happen to be those who do not have the talent of being great.

Cheap inventions are as unpardonable in industry and every-day life as they are in the art galleries. Modernists may scoff at tradition, denouncing it as affectation, old-hat habit, or revolt against change, but real art and tradition have a very close association. Planned obsolescence and invention just for the sake of change are constant causes for public concern with modern industrial design.

I have long admired the simple beautiful curve of the early American reaping hook. It is so delicate and precise that I find it nearly impossible to duplicate in a painting, so on several occasions I traced it from an original implement. Yet, to my amazement, all ancient hooks, though hand-forged by different early American farmers from Maine to the southlands, have the same exact, unique curve. This was a case of traditional acceptance, willingness to confess satisfaction, and man's decision to stay with perfection. Such a simple farm tool, in my belief, could be exhibited as fine American art with more meaning and reason for being in an American museum than most of the things you might see there.

The *great* artist is like a great actor, while the *clever* artist is like a vaudevillian, showman, or clown—bright, dexterous, quick, talented, appealing largely to our sense of humor. A giant hot-water bag or a giant tennis shoe or a soup can such as modern critics have hailed as fine museum art are fair examples of such cleverness. Even the art expert falls victim to contagious cleverness and so produces magnificently clever mumbo jumbo. For example, I quote from a leading American modern-art magazine in which the expert editor commented upon a "black on black" that was virtually a framed black canvas void of any work at all.

"This is a pivotal work of the artist," he wrote, "for in the context of abstract-expressionist noise and gesture, it suddenly brings you face to face with a numbing, devastating silence. Even granting the salvational overtones, an implication that no work at all has been done, no expected artistry has been demonstrated, this leaves the viewer with himself and the magnificent void in front of him. His shadow moves across the blank screen and mirrors the stammering images of an unwilling mind. The

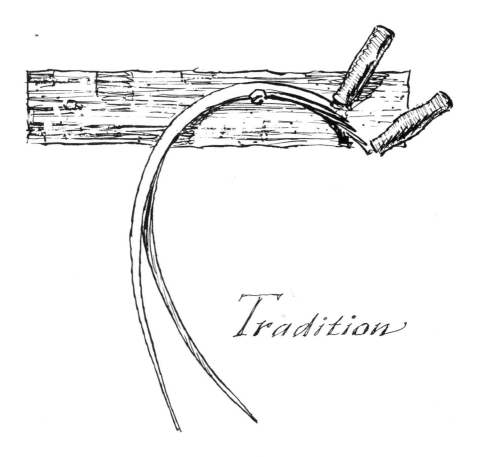

beauty of nothingness and the absence of movement here is magnificent."

Reading that, an intelligent person hardly knows whether to laugh or cry; the complacent American accepts it with a laugh because cleverness often calls for a laugh. In this case, however, I cry.

Once upon a time after painting a giant cloudscape of the sky at night, I set upon the work of painting in stars on the field of blue-black. That was when I had an undue respect for cleverness and (may I be forgiven) decided to title that painting "Diamonds in the Sky"; then the idea struck me that as no one had ever done so, I would continue to be clever and insert *real* diamonds! I suppose I valued publicity and so decided to keep my idea secret until the last strategic moment; actually I should have kept it secret even unto myself, for after purchasing a number of fine diamonds and having them all mounted and set into my painting, I found that they didn't sparkle as I thought they would. In fact they looked black. Even with a spotlight, they didn't show up as brilliant as simple white paint would. The whole idea was a dismal mistake, but there might have been a moral involved, perhaps that any idea at all is worth a try. Or there might be some sort of meaning in the fact that when I later took the gems back for a refund, the value of diamonds had so risen that I earned more than I would have by just selling the painting.

It seems to take much effort from the gods for me to learn my lessons because I later did another "clever" painting. A madcap friend named Henry Morgan built a home on Cape Cod, near a lighthouse, and I gave him as a house present a painting of the nearby shore and "his" lighthouse. Of course, when he turned on a tiny switch in the frame and the lighthouse began casting a powerful electric beam, he was delighted. Perhaps I shall never really learn.

One day while six stories up on my scaffold doing the cloud mural in the Smithsonian's Air and Space Museum, two flouncy art experts appeared from the very modern and very fashionable Hirshhorn Museum next door. "It is absolutely *exquisite!*" said one to the other. "This should be in the Hirshhorn Museum representing American art instead of being here in an aviation museum." I leaned over from my lofty perch. "Thank you, gentlemen," I said. "Oh my!" one of them exclaimed. "We didn't know you were working up there! We really weren't talking about your work—we were just referring to the scaffold."

Overhearing what people say about you may be embarrassing, but it can also be as valuable as it is amusing, and so I always enjoy such eavesdropping at my exhibitions. One old New Englander went to see my work. "You are lucky," said the gallery director. "Would you like to meet the artist?" The old fellow looked about, thought deeply, and replied with typical New England brevity. "Nope," he said.

A lady inspected a large Sloane cloudscape with a tiny spot of a plane in it. She read the title, "Flying at Forty Thousand," and turned to her companion. "Good Lord," she exclaimed. "That's higher than Wyeth gets!" Two young experts once chatted at a gallery show. "Did you ever hear of this Eric Sloane person?" asked one. "Oh sure," the other replied. "But he really isn't *that*

Scaffold·Sculpture

good." A frequent gallery question has been, "Is this the *ashcan* Sloane?" and one remark that always makes me groan is "What beautiful frames!" Now and then someone reads my signature and asks another what N.A. means, and the reply is "I guess it means *non-abstract.*" I collected enough of these eavesdroppings to fill a book, but throughout the years I have been satisfied to keep them only as personal mementos. I recall one unforgettable and touching comment spoken by a very old New England countryman who was viewing a show of my early farm scenes. There was a tear in his eye and so I moved closer to catch any remark he might make; when he spoke, it was a gem. He said aloud but still as if talking to himself, "I wish my wife were alive!"

A painter can labor so diligently at his work that soon he becomes blind to the small mistakes that craftsmanship covers and disguises. Seldom does a painter view his own work later without discovering tiny errors or things that he would have done differently. A museum attendant once found such a man touching up one of the paintings displayed on the gallery wall. When the police arrived, the man explained that he was "only the artist" and, wanting the museum to have a perfect example of his work, was correcting what he considered a small error. When I do a painting that I am fairly satisfied with (a rare happening), it is my custom to hang it in my own gallery for a week or a month; every now and then the painting gets back to my easel for some small change. Often that small change evolves into so many other changes that I finally destroy the whole piece and start again from scratch. Perhaps someday I shall do something that satisfies me completely, but I hope not, for at that point I'd be too easily satisfied.

There is one painting by a famous Hudson River School artist hanging in a great museum that someday I might change (if nobody sees me do it). That painting originally hung in my living room. It was a New England landscape that (to me) cried out for a typical church spire in the tree-shrouded distance; so, one day, unable to stand the omission, I added a tiny white steeple. I won't mention the name of the artist now because I am ashamed of my forgery. Especially so when the museum art critic pointed out the "typical religious theme of the early American masters. That faraway spire," he wrote, "is the final touch of this painter's rare genius." I rather think the artist would turn over in his

grave and not only forgive me, but with a chuckle thank me.

Even though realism (in its many forms) has been the true art since the beginning of civilization, it is only now beginning to be accepted as a "popular movement" in art. Abstractionism, Cubism, Fauvism, Dadaism, and so on along the unending eccentric path of modern art are the real diversions and movements of revolt. When tradition ends, revolutionary minds try desperately to create something to take its place. Waldo Frank reminded us that "in a dying world, *creation* is *revolution*."

Since that Armory Show of 1913, when it was discovered that shock and fad had extraordinary art appeal, the critics have continued to awe the man in the street with abstract rhetoric, and art galleries have been selling more prestige than art. Yet that ridiculed and well-known man in the street who claims to "know nothing about art but only knows what he likes" commands my deep respect. I believe strange and unintelligible art cannot represent American culture, if only for the simple fact that it is not understood by the average American. I believe culture rests with the majority and is never the product of a chosen few.

Culture, like the kingdom of heaven, lies deeply within each of us—not just in galleries or even in books and museums. I agree with Emerson who said that culture is one thing and varnish another, and Whistler who said, "As music is the poetry of sound, so is painting the poetry of sight."

These definitions of art, to my way of thinking, are of greater importance to the student than any other instruction, for the legacy left by the great masters is less their material craftsmanship than their private interpretations of art. Although I have spent much time in schools, I am certain that I have learned more by studying the great painters' definitions of art than I have working in classes at an easel. Anyone, even the uninformed and unlearned, feels the pleasure of art but only the true artist understands the reason; only *he* can define art. Michelangelo regarded a real work of art "the shadow of divine perfection" and Ruskin declared, "All that is good in art is the expression of one soul talking to another, and it is precious according to the greatness of the soul that utters it."

Perhaps there are fewer great people than there used to be; there are certainly more who *think* they are great. Artists and actors and singers and athletes are more and more measured by their salaries: paintings are measured by what grand prices they bring instead of what grand emotions they evoke. The American Ashcan school was a proud group of revolutionists but I wonder how proud they would be viewing the present day course of their revolution.

Being a painter is a rare privilege. It is a way of life with a personal reward far beyond anything that business has to offer. The next thing to living one's life over is to make durable recollections of it, and that, for me, is the personal adventure of being a painter.

Untitled, mixed media.

The Adventure of Writing

My first book for Funk & Wagnalls was supposed to be about weather vanes, but it turned out to be about covered bridges. "What about our contract for a weather-vane book?" asked my publisher. "When I went to New England to research weather vanes," I told him, "I discovered wooden bridges instead." Mr. Cuddihy had a keen sense either of humor or of business because he said, "That's okay with me." That was over twenty-five years ago and the book sells better now than it did then, so I guess we did the right thing. Publishers like that went out of style when the computers took over.

Some writers begin a book with its title. Then (because publishers like it that way) they make a detailed outline with appropriate chapters. The only thing left from there on is to fill in the missing words. However, my method (like the way I paint without preliminary sketches or even a charcoal outline and let the painting finish itself) is to write as if thinking aloud on paper. I never know what I am going to think next, and it is a private and constant astonishment to see thoughts that come from nowhere collecting on paper and making poetic sense.

I have always believed that we all do things differently, but with proper effort, anyone can do anything. Emerson said that all men are poets at heart, and because a poem need not say anything or mean anything, just writing your name is a good start. The only thing wrong with most poets is that they try too hard to be poets.

When I wrote *A Reverence for Wood,* I tried to find appropriate short poems by famous writers to head each chapter of the book, but when I came to the chapter about firewood, I could not find anything suitable. When the publisher's deadline arrived and still no poem had been found, I decided to write one. Of course, I didn't want to attribute it to "Eric Sloane" but I did want to be honest, so I signed my real name, Everard Hinrichs:

> The heft and feel of a well-worn handle,
> The sight of shavings that curl from a blade;
> The logs in the woodpile, the sentiment of huge beams in
>   an old-fashioned house;
> The smell of fresh-cut timber and the pungent fragrance
>   of burning leaves;
> The crackle of kindling and the hiss of burning logs.
> Abundant to all the needs of man, how poor the world
>   would be
> Without wood.
>
> Everard Hinrichs

I am still getting letters asking who this poet Hinrichs is, and my one and only poem was even given a literary prize. Believe me, anyone can do anything.

Writing should never be considered a business; it is speaking on paper, emoting on paper, remembering on paper. Seeing my thoughts and recollections appear in manuscript form is adequate compensation, so I don't really care whether someone buys my words or not, and I believe that is exactly how it should be. Free-lance writing is free-lance thinking and there is something independent and American in such pursuit.

In ancient times, a mercenary soldier whose arrow and lance and military services were available for any cause whatsoever was known as a "free-lance." Nowadays a writer who isn't on salary is called a "free-lance writer" and there is still a certain stigma to that title.

It doesn't seem so long ago that I moved to Connecticut and I well remember my first visit to the local bank. All I wanted was a loan of a thousand dollars. "What security do you have?" asked the bank president. "Well," I replied, "I have no material wealth, but my income is constant. I have a few books on the market so far, and I sell a painting now and then." I can still recall his peering over his glasses at me. "Artists and writers," he said, "are insecure. Royalties don't mean a thing to a bank. Now if you can get someone with a steady job to sign a note, I'll consider the loan. A free-lance writer is a bad risk."

Recently one of my publishers sold the company (as is the constant habit in the modern book business) and the editor of that company found himself suddenly without a job. Overnight he was about where he had been when he first started, except when he first started he was young. It made me think about that great American myth *security*.

Security is within, not without; it is essentially a spiritual experience, different for every situation. It is seldom something you can store away in a safe-deposit box. The greatest security on this earth is in free-lance faith, not what someone thinks of you but what you think of yourself. I remember when putting royalty checks into my savings account was an accomplishment of security, but the government seeks security too, and the fifty percent bracket puts you in a national partnership. Now I find more security in ideas and notes and quotations that I copy down at random; I put those in the safe deposit of my mind: The interest is both enormous and nontaxable.

As with painting, I believe that writing, too, is a communication of recollections—that true art is the moving portrayal of remembrances and that the writer with the greatest remembrances is the real artist among authors.

Once upon a time long ago, I lived in the studio of a painter named Leon Gaspard who specialized in portraying the Mongolian scene, although his studio was in Taos, New Mexico. The New Mexican Indians, their ponies, and the surrounding landscapes all reminded Gaspard of his faraway Mongolian subjects and he found that painting from memory aroused more powerful spirits than could painting from actual life. "I see better with my memory," he said. At that time I did not know what he meant, but I now realize that a man carries with him his personal thesaurus of remembrances and recollections, locked in memory, like a reference library.

Recently I returned to Taos after half a century of New England and instead of portraying the Southwest, I found myself painting and writing about faraway Connecticut. I had become a hopeless New Englander, and although the New Mexican skies and landscapes are incomparable, I felt like Thoreau in Palm

Beach, without inspiration, bored by good weather. Now when I want to paint or write about a southwestern scene, I go back to my weather-beaten Connecticut and observe New Mexico from the adventures of my mind, where the pictures are always most vivid and colorful.

Life consists of what a man is thinking all day and as I regard writing as thinking on paper, it is difficult for me not to write. I know what Disraeli meant when he said, "When I want to read a book, I write one," and I have found that the best (and most enjoyable) way for me to learn something is to write a book about it. The result is that the student who reads such a book has the comfortable feeling that he is thinking and learning *with* you. (Of course, he is doing just that, but you must not let him know! Even if you told him, he wouldn't believe you.) Old-fashioned Horace said that "knowledge is the foundation of good writing," but practical Emerson said that "knowledge is the knowing that we cannot know," and I agree mostly with him.

In these purposeless years of abstract expression, purposeful writing has lost appeal; reading for amusement has become an escape. But being hopelessly old school in my convictions, I believe that life and its arts should exist for definite and good reasons. My main reason for writing has been with the purpose of retrieving certain worthwhile things of the American past that I believe have been foolishly discarded. The reason for this particular book is obvious by its title.

Authority has never been my most respected master: I have often been amused when I find myself quoting myself as an authority. One time, when seeking knowledge about the history of building American barns, the New York Public Library had difficulty in helping me find proper material. Finally, the librarian came up with three books she thought would enlighten me. "They should answer your questions. They are all written by an authority," she said, "named Eric Sloane."

A university that seemed to consider me an accepted American writer recently asked me to contribute "an instructive piece" for their journal. Asking me to offer advice to students about learning how to write might have been a mistake. My reply could not be at all what they expected, for *I do not believe writing can be taught.* The arts may be furthered by instruction, but the writer's best teacher (I believe) is always the writer himself. I suppose that shocked them.

May I explain that shock treatment is my personal method (deplored by my critics), but if you have talent, neither shock treatment nor anything else will discourage you as a writer. So, not considering it advice, may I be only a commentator, relating my own methods for you to utilize or discard as you see fit.

No worthwhile writing ever began by the author sitting down before a piece of paper. There is nothing more defeating than blank paper accompanied by a blank mind. No two people think or work alike but my own writing occurs best while I am operating a car, building a stone fence, painting a house, falling asleep, doing *anything* except actually trying to write. Perhaps some authors' thoughts give a loud knock on the front door and enter like lusty salesmen. My thoughts, however, seem to sneak in from nowhere; suddenly I find them sitting quietly alongside me, and I am never sure how long they've been there. Man is a thinker, but his great works are often done when he is not calculating or thinking.

Actually, "seeking an idea" is unnecessary, for it is usually the idea that seeks *you*. Life is crowded with ideas seeking writers for expression. Eric Hatch was a famous author. His book *My Man Godfrey* won honors as a motion picture, but he fell upon a confused period in his life when he "could not come up with ideas for writing." He even spent some time with psychiatry in search of a remedy. My house happened to be located on the way to his psychiatrist and Eric used to stop by for coffee and a chat. "Anyone who goes to a psychiatrist," I always told him, "needs his head examined," but Eric insisted his "author's think-tank" had just gone stale. "All right," he said, "tell me how *you'd* go about it."

"While I make coffee," I told him, "sit at the window and just look out. When I come back, tell me what you saw." I returned with coffee in a few minutes. "The only thing that commanded my attention," Eric said, "is that brass bell by your driveway." "There's your answer," I told him, and Eric's first book after ten years was his *Little Book of Bells.* His psychiatrist began missing an interesting patient.

I found the same thing true with painting, letting ideas float in at random; paying more attention to faraway daydreaming than to what you are doing often produces a most satisfactory work. I used to be annoyed with interrupting telephone calls, but now I have a telephone attached to my easel. I have learned to paint while carrying on conversations, and when a telephone call has ended, I am often surprised at what has happened on my easel. Some of my best work has evolved into what I call my telephone paintings, works of art that "paint themselves."

One way to let my mind wander away and allow it to express itself is to work while listening to music. Of course, there is music that lulls, causing us to think eloquently, and then there is what they call "modern" music, which might be better accompaniment to an epileptic fit; it does the opposite to me from what I believe music should do. If you are a genius, there's only one thing better to work by and that is absolute silence, but I'm no genius and the lilting strains of music bring out the best in my humble imagination. As for jazz, I agree with corny Sousa that it will endure as long as people hear it through their feet instead of their brains.

When I was young, the world seemed full of sentiment and emotion; now sentiment has changed to callousness and emotion has erupted into violence. Much modern music, to my mind, reflects exactly that change. I've tried in vain to find a satisfactory tape of those soothing old-time melodies—"music to think by." One just came out, but advertised by the title of "Mom and Pop Music." I refused to lower myself and buy such an insult to my music appreciation. I suppose Bach's music is really better than it sounds (to me), but the soul-stirring strains of yesterday's songs seem to bring the most tears to my eyes and the richest words to my typewriter.

A number of years ago while renting a studio in Taos to try my hand at writing, I enjoyed an old phonograph with a "morning glory" horn attached. The musical *Rosemarie* had just appeared in New York and all the way to New Mexico my mind had been haunted by the strains of "Indian Love Call." With that music as a background, I felt that writing would come easy for me, so off I went to buy the record in Albuquerque, a round trip of about two hundred and fifty miles. There I found my music, a recording by someone (I'd not yet heard of) named Artie Shaw.

I set the old phonograph beside my writing desk and breathlessly waited to hear my theme song. "When you hear my call, boop de doop, bangety bang," came the ragtime rape of my favorite air, "Then you'll know my secret, wham de bang boopety boop!" I suppose I was more emotional in those days. Before I could stand further disgrace to my song, I snatched the record and flung it through both window and screen.

When I went to my landlord, Mr. Gaspard, to confess my rash act and offer to pay him for the damage, he seemed more amused than annoyed. "Never mind," he said. "I would have done the same thing." Gaspard was a true artist.

Writing to compete (like writing to make money) is both bad manners and bad thinking: Being yourself and enjoying your writing is paramount. Nowadays competition is the major philosophy of business, the backbone of the national economy, and the essence of sports. Competition is the spark of the American way. Yet no doctor, inventor, painter or writer ever reached greatness by means of competition. The only person that any kind of artist should compete with should be himself. Always trying to do better work used to be the rule of old-time writers, but that was when there was such a thing as indecency and four-letter words were considered crude or rude. Now a popular author depends on spice. Sensationalism is king, and writing has become a competitive industry instead of an art and a way of life.

Perhaps I am an incurable curmudgeon who lives in the past, but I find so many instances of the old ways, the old times and people, being more genuine than they are today. I remember going to the old Funk & Wagnalls offices in downtown New York and going to the president's office (which had no door) to explain that I needed a couple of thousand dollars plus fifty copies of this book and a hundred copies of another from my list. "Where is your car parked?" president Cuddihy would say. And in a matter of minutes I left with my check and a carload of books, a happy author.

Now the publishing houses are uptown, the whole staff seems in a constant Madison Avenue turmoil of conferences, and actual books are stored in warehouses a hundred or more miles away. Computers have taken the place of editors or accountants with whom a writer could speak. The romance of producing literature is gone and publishing has become a hectic business.

Old-time publishers even had a sense of humor. When Walt Disney wrote to me and asked if I'd sell my book *Diary of an Early American Boy* for a thousand dollars, I was indignant at first. Then I wrote to Mr. Disney. "I know how my unhappy friend the author of *Ferdinand the Bull* realized a like sum from you, yet I also know what a great job you do. I'd be proud to have you produce my book on the screen; I'd even *pay you* for doing it, instead of selling my life's work for so little. You might as well offer me a couple of dollars as a lousy thousand; that, perhaps, I'd accept!" In my bathroom where I hang my trophies is Disney's famed reply with a check for two dollars from Walt Disney Productions.

Just as competition turns out shoddy automobiles, the competing author turns out shoddy writing, and so today's world of books is infested with a sea of verbal garbage. I would rather choose an author exactly as I would choose a friend or companion (not someone competing for my acceptance) and the writer whose language would be out of place in my living room is not welcome in my library. Vulgarity in writing and selling cheap sex in book form is one way of making a living, but it still makes the author a pimp. Good taste is an aspect of genius; even Shakespeare, whose words were often coarse, reminded the writer to "be familiar, but by no means vulgar."

Not composed completely at the typewriter, my writing is more often molded together with scrap paper, rubber cement, and scissors. I keep a pad at my bedside to capture thoughts that might escape before morning, for I am hopelessly superstitious about how the answers to life's questions seem to come to me best while in a horizontal position. I have often gone to bed wondering about some literary problem, which is answered miraculously just before I open my eyes in the morning. My studio equipment always includes a couch. When thoughts and words stumble over each other, I lie down. But there is seldom time for even a minute nap because almost the instant I assume that contemplative position I bounce back to the typewriter with cleared thinking, the answer delivered. Actually, there is nothing miraculous about this, for prolonged sitting does rob the head and brain of some blood circulation, and a sudden change to a reclining position does tend to activate it again.

Among my other beliefs is the conviction that prayers are really answered. I am not a churchgoer but some of my methods are quite Baptist. I believe that the re-creative mind is constantly making infinitesimal prayers, that the painter, for example, is constantly asking: Is *this* the right color? Is *this* shape too severe? Should I add a highlight *here* or *there?* And I believe all these small wonderments are answered, but it takes alertness and awareness to recognize the heavenly replies. The miraculous answers arrive in strange ways, so they must be watched for. Believe it or not, if a tube of paint falls while I am working at my easel, I might consider that as an answer and so I try to use that very color. This has been working for me for over half a century, so I care little what anyone thinks. It is an exciting and not unpleasant kind of madness. The same phenomena, then, occur while writing. If I have trouble with a thought, if the answer doesn't come, I take a walk, have a cup of coffee or work on my stone fence, and in some miraculous way my prayer is answered. Perhaps that was what Susan B. Anthony had in mind when she said, "I pray every single second of my life; not on my knees, but with my work, and God replies." Few successful writers consider their work a spiritual accomplishment, yet writing is the poetry of thought and the author is no more than an outlet for infinite intelligence. Perhaps that is what Emerson had in mind when he said, "All writing comes by the grace of God."

I type with five-line spaces, which is seldom enough room to accommodate all the changes and corrections. One short Sloane sentence that sounds carefree and flippant, spontaneous and off-the-cuff, might be the result of fifty tries with scissors and rubber cement and as many contributions to the wastebasket. That sort of writing may be little inspiration and loads of perspiration but it is always worth the trouble. And it is always worthy of a five-second "time-out" for thanks to my Teacher; He deserves that.

When my wife changes my writing or contests my thoughts in any way, I raise Cain. I argue, squirm, and finally prove that my way was really right and that I know best. Then I quietly consider her point and I make the change. But don't think I'm a henpecked writer—I always put up a loud and proper fuss! What I'm trying to say is that the critic is a necessary evil and criticism is an evil necessity; I never belittle criticism, for as dirty a name as I may call criticism at the time, it is still a most valuable manure to my garden of thoughts.

I deplore people who read "to pass away the time"; they usually read books written by authors who write for the same reason. I feel there should be a good reason for *reading*, but there should always be a better reason for *writing*. A writer is not someone who writes as much as someone who thinks, and the writer's prime reason for being is to help others think. Teaching people to think is the highest calling of civilization.

Writing is an apparatus for the conveyance of thought. Some writers write because they have something to say; others write just because they want to say something. The writer who writes for the purpose of making money should forget it; there are easier ways to make a living. When you chase money, it becomes elusive, but when you ignore it for the love of hard work, money seeks you out like a neglected lover: Payments will come in from stuff you had even forgotten about. Writing shouldn't be a commercial occupation, because it is a religion and a calling that should never be treated sacrilegiously.

I write involuntarily, like an exercise that I can't help doing. When writing (or painting) becomes a job, my life becomes empty and without pleasure. There is always that question, "which would you rather do—paint or write?" and I'd really rather not think about choosing one over the other. A thought put in words, however, might take weeks of agony, of discarding and changing, of embellishing and philosophizing into the night. Writing is a lengthy procedure, but the results are gratifying. A painting done in only an hour or two might earn twice as much as a whole book, yet a book is never confined to someone's wall, it never fades, and many years later, it speaks as freshly as when it was written. You can tell the age of a painting; written words are ageless. As for me, I regard my paintings as illustrations of my thoughts. So I guess my writing comes first.

I remember staying with an Amish family in Pennsylvania and offering them a small oil painting as a house present. After refusing the gift, my host reminded me of their religious habit of avoiding any kind of decoration. "An artist would have a difficult time around here," I commented, but the old fellow took me to his bedroom. There over the bed was a framed piece of Fraktur lettering, spelling out the word LOVE. "Confucius said that one picture is worth a thousand words," he said solemnly, "but here is one word worth a thousand pictures."

Secluded

The Adventure of Being Alone

I find comfort and peace in solitude. When alone, I am actually protected against loneliness. There are those who would live by the side of the road and watch the race of man go by, but my idea of a perfect place to live is a farmstead where I can't see another house. Even a distant chimney shatters my sense of tranquility; at night, faraway lit windows are prying eyes watching me.

You can tell a "loner" by his work: a writer who enjoys being alone writes as if talking to himself and the same sort of painter views landscapes without benefit of people to enliven the scene. My countryside subjects seldom have anyone there, and for a while I wondered if I had lost the knack of painting people. When Louis Nizer spoke in presenting an art award to me, he brought that up and I squirmed. "Sloane seldom has people in his paintings," he said. Then that man talented with the gift of words delighted me. "But there is always someone in Sloane's paintings," he added. "It is *you!*"

I see nothing eccentric about being a loner, but there are those who resent the recluse and consider his seclusion an effrontery and an intentional offense to society. When I first moved to the country and the real-estate agents kept showing me "secluded houses" surrounded by neighbors, I tried to explain my idea of privacy. "What I want," I stated, "is a place so alone that I can run around the house naked without anyone around to see me. I want to be able to shoot a gun in all directions without even being in *range* of another house." I thought that would tell the story. But I soon began to notice people nudging each other and viewing me suspiciously. "There goes that man," they'd whisper, "who runs around his house naked, shooting off guns."

Knowing the difference between *alone* and *lonely* can be more important than other things a student learns in this life, and when I think of the time I spent with Latin, I wonder why the simple study of living was never considered a proper school subject. The amazing number of recent dropouts, runaways, and teen-age suicides might indicate the need for children to know the fine art of coping with being alone.

Nowadays I am constantly amazed to see homework or serious school reading being done in a room throbbing with the discord of psychedelic music, and I wonder how anyone can concentrate at all when surrounded by an electrified stereo band. Yet students say it keeps them from being lonely!

One can feel alone in the busiest conglomeration of people. New York loneliness is a particularly insidious strain of the disease, and watching people riding the subway or walking along the streets, you will find blank masks stamped with depression. Faces are more alive in the morning rush, but by noon the glow has lessened. When day is done and the buildings begin to empty, the desolate pilgrimage home becomes a huge parade of loneliness. Being alone and lonely are two things very far apart.

There are still a few who try crossing the ocean solo in tiny boats, but Lindbergh was probably the last of the great era of lone adventurers. Nowadays most sports are "group" or "contact" or "competitive," but I can remember when skiing and hiking and sailing and canoeing were particularly exciting when done solo. An athletic fad at the turn of the century required a participant to enter a forest alone, without any clothing or equipment, combat the challenge of weather and hunger; and return to civilization well-fed and clothed in animal skins. The lone sportsman knew he had won. About a hundred men did this remarkable feat in the early 1900s, then wrote books about their experience. (There is a story about one woman who did it and returned in a mink coat but I think that was just a shaggy mink story.)

There are still a few sports where the danger and thrill is heightened doing it all by yourself, like ballooning, parachute jumping, and gliding. One soaring pilot commented upon the awesomeness of silence and solitude. "When you are alone up there," he said, "you realize more than ever *who* you are and *why* you are. It may sound crazy, but I get my spiritual nourishment from this sport."

Being alone has a humanizing effect, causing personality to be uninhibited and making the human mind more communicative. Even in writing, when an author writes in the first person, he immediately feels as if he is alone, speaking aloud but expressing himself more freely and directly to the reader.

As you walk along a crowded street, you usually pass people without a communicative glance, but on a quiet street when you approach a solitary person coming the opposite way, you will find yourself nodding, even saying hello, and you will find yourself greeted likewise. I recall hiking across a prairie and seeing someone nearly a mile off heading only roughly in my direction. When a quarter mile off, we both felt called upon to head closer, wave a greeting, and then approach each other. Our paths finally merged, we introduced ourselves, chatted and then continued separately on our way. Actually, it was a strange performance provoked by the unexplainable magnetism of two people being alone.

One whose frequent companion is solitude, a hermit in the cave of his own mind, the writer is often a lonely person. But loneliness can also be a sweet suffering; and suffering, so they say, makes one more sincere. Such a sincere writer was Van Wyck Brooks, who knew New England well. He once asked me if I enjoyed my move from the city and I told him how the country produced a strange loneliness that I actually enjoyed. "That," he said, "makes you old-school American. Loneliness is particularly evident on the New England face; it is the American bittersweet of pain and pleasure. But those who live understandingly with it," he added, "find it a tolerable and even exciting companion." I knew what he meant, for I have since enjoyed the loneliness of New England hills, that rambling melancholy of deserted farms and stone-fence monuments of other days. In the most stirring autumn landscape, I still sense a pleasant echo of nostalgic contemplation.

Solitude in youth is painful because the art of living comfortably with it has not yet been learned; it is usually only in maturity that solitude becomes delicious. At one time, whenever life was confusing and my mind lacked decision, I immediately went to knowledgeable people for advice, but I have since learned that the answers were usually within me all the while. Now when I am perplexed, I seek seclusion, and in the eloquence of silence, I just wait for the replies to arrive. And they do.

In solitude we are least alone because we are in the presence of cosmic mind, and if there be a God, He speaks loudest when we are alone. One Navaho chant translates that philosophy into Indian poetry: *Only in silence do you hear the gods whisper.*

A very long while ago, when I painted signs for a living, I spent one whole winter in Coney Island painting the carousels in Steeplechase Amusement Park. The rides were within a giant block-long room, which was remembered best in summer, noisy and crowded with vacationists. When it became an enormous quiet icebox during winter, closed and empty, the stillness therein became unbearable, for the place, haunted with the din of summertime noise, screeched with a loud silence that you felt instead of heard. My portable radio helped to dispel that strange discomfort and when I forgot to bring the radio, I often found myself singing at the top of my lungs. George Tilyou, who owned the park, was anything but a pious fellow and he usually visited the place during winter on Sundays. "It's so quiet in here," he told me, "I come here so I can think things out. I find it better than going to church."

I was introduced to the fascination of being alone at an early stage. Having run away from home to work on a remote Pennsylvania farm with Hans and Hilda Appelbaum, I knew well what it meant to be homesick; they spoke only German and I knew nothing of their language. After supper in the evening we would sit on the porch and listen to all the living sounds of summer and make occasional vague attempts at conversation. They spoke in pidgin English, I in broken German. The language barrier lessened a bit one night when Hilda pointed into the darkness and called attention to the droning of an insect known thereabouts as the *lonesome bug*. "*Vass ist dass?*" she asked. Then I tried to act out the word "lonesome": I feigned tears, tried to look forlorn, and I uttered what I thought were lonesome sounds. She got the point. "*Ach!*" she exclaimed. "*Dass ist ein heimveh* [homesick] *bugg!*" I will always remember making "lonely faces" for Hans

and Hilda, trying to explain that being alone was some sort of dread disaster. Now, at my age, to mimic solitude I would most likely smile broadly and try to look very contented.

Old-style Europeans understand *homesickness* well, because of their typical closely knit family life, and for the same reason they experience very little *loneliness*. In America, homesickness was once a common ailment, but nowadays you hear nothing about it. You will hear countless kidlets strumming guitars and singing about being *lovesick*, but I have yet to hear one of them sing about being homesick, missing ma and pa and the old homestead. The reason is that there are fewer established homes in America nowadays. That sounds like an idiotic statement but it is a fact that today the average home is only temporary shelter. A century ago homes were built for your children and your children's children. I recall living in six houses before I became of age, several apartments as a young man, and eleven houses that I more recently built or remodeled; each place (for a while) was what I called my home. I didn't stay long enough in any of them to ever be homesick.

I remember watching the demolition of an early Pennsylvania stone house. The old building was made by a plain "unskilled" farmer in 1740, but taking it down required a small army of expert workers and two giant bulldozers. The tremendous granite cornerstone must have taken a few oxen to put in place and it had a small inscription scratched into it: GOTT BAUT FÜR DIE EWIGKEIT (God builds for Eternity). Eternity, however, is reserved for God and so "forever" can be a very short time for man. The family homestead has already become vanished American history and so has homesickness. Loneliness lingers on.

the Adventure of being a

Collector

If you find a pair of rare items you are lucky; if you find a third, you're on your way to being a collector. Once in an antique shop, for no other reason than conversation, I looked at a very large rectangular wooden bowl and remarked to my wife, "Isn't this an interesting piece?" To her, that meant I could hardly live another moment without it, so Christmas came and so did the very large rectangular wooden bowl. I had neither room nor use for the thing, but it intrigued me because I couldn't imagine how anyone else could have had room for it or what they would have used it for. So every antiquarian I visited, I made inquiry. I asked in about a hundred antique shops, and to my surprise, ten of them had nearly identical bowls which never sold. Each was priced much lower than mine, so I felt compelled to take advantage of such a bargain and I now own eleven very large rectangular wooden bowls. I am still trying to learn what the confounded things were used for, but I certainly hope I find no others. Those bowls are destined for my museum; the life of a collector is usually cluttered with his collections and they become most valuable only when given away.

The process of collecting involves three separate senses: *instinct, opinion,* and *knowledge.* You are born with instinct and you can soon develop opinion, but knowledge is a slow process reserved for only the few. There are also three closely related joys that, when you become aware of them, enrich the collector's life. They are the adventures of *finding*, of *collecting*, and of *giving*. All three are of equal pleasure and satisfaction, but one without the others tends to create a certain poverty. For example, the man who *finds* gold experiences profound joy; then, *collecting* his riches produces pleasure and satisfaction (which in time becomes boring), but an *exactly equal* pleasure and satisfaction comes with giving it all away! Even my accountant agrees with that idea, for he spends much of his time figuring what I can give away. This rule of three is something every collector should consider from the beginning.

I remember the excitement I had in finding an early American broadaxe in a stone fence behind my barn; it led me to searching all the rest of my stone fencing around the place and I soon came up with a sizeable collection of cast-off rusty implements, which I cleaned and mounted on exhibition boards. Before long I had a barnful of old tools and not long after that, I had written a book about them. Then I donated my entire collection to the state of Connecticut, all housed in a barnlike structure in Kent. That rounded out the threefold process of *finding, collecting,* and *giving,* and it was one of the few adventures I have had in my life that I am completely proud of. As important, however, was the *fun* of doing all three things.

Often when visiting the museum, my eye is caught by a certain tool; it is that first axe, which I found in the stone fence. I always pause in greeting, neither one of us actually speaking, of course, but there seems to be a profound acknowledgment of an eloquent and satisfying association.

Anyone can buy treasures, but the joy of finding them is what really makes the incurable collector. Many years ago I had a friend named Captain Doudera who owned the Balsams Hotel in New Hampshire. When I did a small mural for him and insisted upon asking no remuneration from so close a friend, he offered me all the paintings he had stored away in his attic. In those days I had not yet heard of Cropsey and Inness and Cole and others of the Hudson River School that were represented in the Captain's attic, so I settled on only one painting in a large gold frame. "I really don't want the *painting*," I explained, "but I do want the frame to sell to a neighbor who needs one for a mirror." The Captain insisted that it was too much trouble to remove the canvas and stretcher. "Take the painting along too," he said.

I sold the frame to my neighbor for a hundred dollars and then offered the painting itself for the same amount, without success. Later when I showed it to Mr. Newman of The Old Print Shop in New York City, and told him I "might take fifty for it," I guess he misunderstood me. "You'll never get fifty for it," he said, "but I think I can get you half that amount. *Twenty-five* thousand would be tops." It sold.

Collectors' stories always seem to go on and on. Another time, while having a Pepsi-Cola in a dingy little luncheon place, I noticed a very dirty and torn painting over the soda fountain. It was so black with soot that it was difficult to ascertain exactly what the subject was, but finally I saw the exact same subject of Captain Doudera's painting, carriage, horses, schoolhouse and all, but with the whole composition reversed. "What is that painting?" I asked. "Oh, that's an old picture someone gave me years ago. Someday I'll get around to throwing it away." I gulped: "I'll give you a hundred dollars for it." He hastened outside for a ladder and soon, with my new treasure, I sped back to The Old Print Shop. Harry Newman was astonished. "Lightning seldom strikes twice," he said, "but I think you've done it again! It's definitely by the same painter!" Evidently it was the reverse of the first painting, a bit larger but unsigned and unfinished. I stupidly offered to "sign it and add hands to the ladies, straps to the baggage, and reins to the horses." Newman, of course, was horrified at my suggestion and insisted it would sell (unfinished and unsigned) at a price similar to that of the first painting. He was absolutely right, for it is now the center of interest in Vermont's Shelburne Museum. The collector is always waiting for lightning to strike twice and the gods are always receptive.

Collecting, like writing or painting or any other art of living, should be more a way of life than a business. The consuming fire of hoarding can soon change a collector into a miser, and he who collects just to make a profit is never an honored member of the brotherhood. One such person was a neighbor, Jon Pol, who gathers everything and possibly has the world's largest collection of thrown-away objects. When I remodel an old house, I always call Jon and quickly manage to get the place cleaned of junk and debris. I noticed in his establishment one day a huge glass jar full of buttons and I recommended that item to a friend who is a button collector. When my friend offered Jon one hundred dollars for his jar of buttons, Jon became dumfounded. But when my friend explained how because of the introduction of zippers, the button is becoming rare and collectable, Jon understood. He regretted selling his jar of buttons, but he soon started collecting zippers. Now he has nicely labeled bags of all kinds of zippers and he is waiting for some future zipper collector to stop by. I'm sure if he lives long enough, that will happen.

I've often written about Jon and I've told that story many times and it always gets a laugh. The picture of him holding those bags of zippers makes him appear so ridiculous; but it turned out differently for Jon. "More people come now just to see my zipper collection," he told me, "and my shop is booming. Thanks to you I have made many friends and I do a very fine business."

As in every large family, the genus *Collectianus* occasionally produces weak or perverse members. A Russian countess paid fabulous sums for the chamber pots of famous historical personages, and a California collector has the underwear of nearly all the movie greats. When Margaret Woodbury Strong died at the age of seventy-two, she had collections of bathtubs, bicycles, thimbles, napkin rings, doorstops, bells, canes, dollhouses, ship models, anvils, hatpins, and a quarter of a million items that earned her the title of world's greatest collector of trivia.

My antiquarian neighbor Norman Flayderman once bought a collection of articles gathered by Napoleon's physician after the Emperor died. The clothing, silver cups, dishes, and bronze death mask were normal collector's items, but an item from his anatomy was an extraordinary part of the collection. Although boxed nicely in a silver case, it is a rather dismal and disappointing exhibit, an item that really doesn't lend itself to additional collecting.

Collecting to make friends may seem farfetched, yet the lonely person who starts collecting immediately wins free membership in an enormous club of prestigious people. The collector with commemorative silver plates in his safe-deposit box may not be aware (or even care) that the actual silver content in his decorative prizes amounts to only half the value that he paid, and that he might have invested more wisely had he bought simple silver bars; the real benefit and joy comes from his membership in the club. A quiet, unassuming fellow of no importance suddenly shares prominence and influence with the renowned when they have similar collecting interests. The director of a major collector-oriented corporation once confided in me: "Between you and me, we are successful because there are so many lonely people in the United States."

Some people think that they are collectors, when actually they are only compulsive gatherers, surrounding themselves with themselves. I suppose we tend to identify ourselves by the things we own. Others collect indiscriminately, gathering old bottles, ceramic elephants or owls, telephone wire insulators, barbed wire, anything, just collecting for the sake of collecting, always in search of the curious and the unique, no matter how ugly or absurd.

The historical significance and spiritual flavor of a collection usually outweighs its material value. Like melting down a Paul Revere piece to sell the silver, the material worth of a collection is usually insignificant. He who collects spiritual memories for his own use is really the richest of collectors. Harry Hirschfield, the great wit and storyteller, lived in a great room crowded with files of letters and mementos of his friends. There were personal letters from American Presidents, starting with Teddy Roosevelt, items from kings and queens and all the greats of his lifetime. Harry slept on a small cot in the middle of the room where he "dreamed about friends." He was far from being lonely. "I meet a better class of people in my dreams," he once told me.

I did find one collector I shall always remember. He collected with exquisite reason and taste, with proud purpose, and with the eye of a true connoisseur. He was a squirrel. He had arranged a fine collection of nuts in my attic. Strangely enough, there were three separate piles of nuts (acorn, hickory, and butternut), and I pondered why an animal would classify his hoard so systematically—why he wouldn't just place them all in one common pile. It robbed me of some sleep. After thinking, however, I decided these three piles represented three separate years of collecting and each pile represented a plentiful year for that particular kind of nut. I have great respect for fellow collectors and so I refrained from disturbing so thoughtful an effort and it still remains in my attic.

I've always thought that, like a marriage ceremony, a divorce should call for some sort of solemn (or at least meaningful) social gesture with toasts to better days and future happiness. After one divorce du jour, a friend had already imbibed quite a bit in such toasts, but the warmth of my fireplace encouraged him to linger and his conversation finally descended to the depths of personal advice. "No wonder a wife can't stand you," he said, waving his hand ceremoniously toward the circumference of my living room. "Every blasted thing here is *you!* Every chair, every table, and each ashtray is something that *you've* collected. You wear your surroundings and furnishings as if they are your own clothes. You don't leave an inch of room for a wife to express herself. I'll bet if she did manage to get some gadget of her own choice in this place, it would disappear in a matter of hours." I looked around the room. He was absolutely right.

That was a long time ago, but I'm still glad my friend reprimanded me and I shall always remember him for it.

Collecting is a private pastime.

Not what Betsy Ross had in mind.

the Adventure of Being an American

"What on earth is that?" I asked my grandchild. "That," he said, "is part of my homework. We learned about Betsy Ross today and the teacher asked all the class to try their hands at designing a new American flag."

The dollar sign could be a commentary on modern America, but it was startling to see it in place of the traditional stars. "The teacher told us how we are a capitalistic nation, so my design tells that story pretty well—don't you think so? Besides," he continued, "if you put the letter U on top of the letter S, it becomes a dollar sign!"

In Russia that sort of thinking about your country might make you eligible for Siberia, but even here, in the land of the free, it seemed to call for some sort of disciplinary teaching. After stumbling around with explanations about bad taste, however, I came to the conclusion that more important than teaching American history, schools should teach exactly what it is to be an American.

The fact that parents regard school and a college diploma as the basis for better jobs and higher earning power stresses the dollar sign in junior's education. Little is taught about the spiritual qualities of being an American. To be a true American is almost a moral condition, and lest we forget that, there should be scholastic reminders.

If you ask any child what he would do with the gift of a billion dollars, his reply is usually that he would "invest it wisely" and the parents smile with pride. In other words, if he were given more money than he would need (or ever have during his whole lifetime), he would plan to earn even *more!* Thought of giving it away quickly and wisely, then earning your own way in life, is never considered nowadays.

From the very beginning we have regarded ourselves as the richest nation on earth but at first, wealth usually didn't refer to money. In fact, once upon a time in America, it was considered rude to dwell upon the subject of money, even crude to mention it. I have a collection of early newspapers that advertise real estate and almost every kind of merchandise you can think of, and there isn't a single mention of price. I also have a collection of early wills, and although household items, land, and other material inheritances are listed meticulously, mention of actual money was rare. The experience of being an American used to be a more spiritual experience than it seems to be now; life and success depended less upon what we had in our wallet. Nowadays a man feels undressed without his wallet, but only a hundred years ago the word "wallet" referred only to a provision bag for clothing (*Webster's Dictionary*, 1878) and men carried but a few emergency coins in a drawstring purse.

Even the words "poor" and "rich" have changed, for both words in the old dictionaries make no mention of money. "Poor" meant "trifling, narrow, mean and without spirit." The same dictionary said that "poor people are without rank and dignity in a community." The word "rich" meant "valuable, precious, the ingredients or qualities of great degree."

Probably no phrase has been used more during the last few decades than "the American heritage," yet asked to define it, few come up with a proper interpretation. It is the title of a magazine and the description of an unending list of household items or "American heritage furniture." Actually, there is hardly a single material thing that we can prove as being American. Once we thought the rocking chair originated here, but Benjamin Franklin really copied it from a Dutch cradle-chair. The only unique American heritage is our spiritual declaration.

The real adventure and heritage of being an American is that you are a member of a club of its own invention. No other organization had yet been founded on the independence of the individual until we invented it and the signers of the great Declaration patented it. We may not regard America as an invention, but a nation dedicated to independence was an invention more important than the electric light, television, or the atomic bomb.

When America was young, there were lofty creeds and absolute trust in God, but our pace has been fast. We have become spiritually tired and we are now experiencing spiritual exhaustion. Our responsibility to God is regarded as obsolete while the need to worship man and material wealth becomes overwhelming. The America we invented was quite different from the America we now live in and according to our best minds, it is vanishing quickly. I do not believe that exactly because instead of the end being near, the end has already come and we have not been aware of it. Our opponent has been complacency and indifference. We have found our enemy and it was us.

What we have today is another America—not what it started out to be but still the greatest thing that man has to offer *if only we accept a rebirth* of the original concept. Even if we should collapse materially, with faith, with the rebirth of our original religious spirits, we would survive. Love, honesty, godliness, hard work, frugality, responsibility, and respect for the individual are more than just Boy Scout qualities; they are the ideals that founded this unique nation. The insidiousness of moral decay leads us to believe these simple values are still with us and are as strong as ever, but when each spirit is looked for in politics and national purpose, the message is loud and clear. We have progressed, but as Lincoln observed over a century ago, "our progress in degeneracy has also been rapid." We do have a very different national purpose than the Founding Fathers intended. Speaking to a clergyman, I decried the modern tendency of recognizing the value of money more than we do our God. He smiled at my panic. "Knowing what is happening to the value of the dollar," he said, "you should know God is doing something about that."

I can hear cries of "Pessimist!" and if I were now lecturing instead of writing, I would most likely be hit by thrown objects. But there is neither pessimism nor optimism in arithmetic; wishfulness will not change a minus sign to a plus sign. The American plan of spending our way into prosperity and the syndrome of have-now-and-pay-later has misinformed us; we cannot enjoy economic growth without first producing it. The Faustian bargain is nearing the final payment.

Thomas Jefferson once compared us with England: "If the debt . . . should be swelled to a formidable size . . . we shall be committed to . . . *debt, corruption* and *rottenness,* closing with *revolution.*" He spoke an awesome truth, for today we have debt (far beyond his "formidable size," even beyond human conception) of about three trillion dollars. Jefferson's "corruption" is also with us in politics, the "rottenness" is with us in pornography, and the "revolution" is with us in violent strikes. His "corruption" and "rottenness" and "revolution" have become an accepted part of everyday America. Debt, that fatal disease of republics, is with us indeed.

Rebirth starts with redeclaration so in praying for a renaissance of the American creed, it seems appropriate to redeclare the original American convictions. Here are those beliefs:

I believe that the moral strength of the nation is exactly as strong as the moral strength of its individuals.

I believe that "In God We Trust" was a profound statement of national commitment and, therefore, democracy without that commitment to God is a departure from the original American concept. Early American patriots were also Christian patriots.

I believe that the same principles that rule the conscience and the economy of the individual also govern the conscience and the economy of the government: I therefore believe that waste in any form is intolerable, and just as no family can long spend more than it earns, neither can a government do so. As frugality is part of family economy, so must it be important to national revenue. The practice of thrift is insurance against greed. Greed had no part whatsoever in the original American philosophy and all evidences of greed now should be abhorred.

I believe that self-dependence produces self-respect. Helping a man to be self-dependent is an admirable pursuit, but helping a man while taking away his initiative and independence is degrading. Permanently doing for a man what he can do for himself is completely contrary and destructive to the original American tradition.

I believe the dignity of work and the foremost pursuit of excellence should be the primary challenge of labor instead of its present constant goal of more pay for fewer hours. That principle is not only decadent to workmanship and demoralizing to the worker but within time becomes logically and financially impossible.

I believe that just as you cannot strengthen the weak by weakening the strong, the wage earner cannot profit by destroying the wage payer. Capital and labor have equal rights in the American system and the independence of both is equally deserving of recognition. For either group to strike against public welfare or violate the innocent is immoral, revolutionary, and against the American tradition.

Dedicated to the dignity of man, having overcome slavery and forever championing human rights, Americans have always been knights in shining armor, but the same knights in business suits have lost moral prestige. After two centuries of incredible scientific development, our spiritual development has suffered. To correct this, our present generation has a rendezvous with destiny even more trying than that of 1776.

In a sense, a total collapse of the dollar would mean an end to the American way, but the nation was not founded on the dollar anyway, so we would still survive. America *was* founded on spiritual principles; only the collapse of those principles could be the end.

The early pioneers were surrounded by threat and danger, too, but they managed to pull through by sheer faith and a rebirth of that same faith is necessary right now. Faith is an inheritance America can never afford to deny and America will endure as long as we have the Lincolnian faith that "this nation under God shall experience a new birth."

I foresee that the adventure of being an American will become an increasingly difficult and trying performance, yet it will also become increasingly more exciting and rewarding. It is going to be hard—after over a century of believing that the purpose of progress is to make life easier—to learn that material progress can mean spiritual decay. The challenge and purpose of life, after all, is not to make life easier but to make man stronger.

The Adventure of Having Lived

... a postscript.

I have never considered the act of cutting down a growing tree and destroying it an appropriate way to celebrate Christ's birthday. So long as I can recall, I have used a live Christmas tree and transplanting it later has always been part of the holy ceremony. The first such tree when I moved from the city to the country was about two feet tall; its trunk was hardly thicker than a pencil and it spent that holiday on my living-room table decorated with candles. Later it went outside, where, to the delight of the winter birds, it was decorated with strings of popcorn.

I still see this tree occasionally, but its girth now is far beyond that of my own body and its uppermost branches tower above all the surrounding trees. I suppose it has become a symbol of revelation to me, and whenever I am in the neighborhood I find myself going out of my way to greet it as I would to greet a comrade.

Looking at myself in a mirror, the anesthesia of slowly passing time disguises the years, but visiting my tree makes me shockingly aware of life lived. I have never had children of my own, but I know what satisfaction a father must have: My giant stepchild has done exceedingly well, fulfilling its purpose as God intended. I hope that I have done as well in His eyes. Few of my old friends remain now, but each time I renew relationship with my tree there is a secret and profound sense of communication and I have the feeling that we compare notes on the adventure of having lived. After a meaningful silence, my pat on its bark skin is as sincere as any handshake with a fellow being.

I find the various lessons in a tree, examples for perfect living. Being of benefit to all other life, being a bible of religious truths and a cathedral of philosophy, a tree is an ideal symbol to mankind. We may think that religious freedom was the prime motive for American pioneering, but another attraction was the wealth of our forests. A tree was pictured on our first flags, there was a tree on our first currency. Before there were churches in America, religious services were held and important charters were always signed beneath some special tree. There was a profound significance in and reverence for wood and trees that seem to be forgotten American history.

Antiquarians often accept the countless things that the old-timers made of wood, the result of metal being scarce. The real fact is that they much preferred wood; they associated their new environment and the qualities of different trees with themselves. If a man was weak, strong, honest or dishonest, he was likened to a certain kind of tree. The American trees were part of life and when the nation was very young, the American surrounded himself with the philosophy of wood. "A tree made into something useful," went an early Puritan saying, "continues to live."

In youth we enjoy the poetry of philosophy for the sheer joy of others' wisdom, but in old age, as we approach the door from which we came, philosophy becomes another matter. It may take a long while, but finally, when we become less influenced by others, man becomes his own philosopher and does his own thinking, dwelling solemnly on the issues of his own past lived.

My own world has been constantly confused by scientists who have delighted in proving that up or down are the same thing and metaphysicians who have propounded that both good and bad are untruths devised only in the mind of man. The recognized logic that there is really no such thing as either beauty or ugliness was a devastating shock to me after spending over half a century in pursuit of beauty and detesting what I thought was ugliness. With respect for the great minds of history, I still believe that the simple knowledge of myself is a surer way to God's truths than deep search into the history of learning: I believe that my mind was created so that I might choose to think my own thoughts. No philosopher's logic can make garbage smell

the Philosophy of Wood

like perfume except to a perverted mentality; no one can prove to me that there is no such thing as good or bad and right or wrong, or that there can be no universal definition of beauty. My definition is: *Beauty consists of all combinations of things in nature, or their reflections in art, that create pleasure and arouse agreeable emotions.*

Nature specializes in beauty, but man specializes in ugliness. We may defile nature, yet if left alone long enough, nature will take over and cover the scars of mankind.

To me, beauty and goodness are synonymous and my own interpretation of both good and beautiful is what I must live by. I believe God is within me and that I exist for the purpose of expressing Him. Such a thought in itself is beautiful and so beauty exists for me and within me.

Like Thoreau, who said "may I gird myself to be a hunter of the beautiful," I want to seek out my own version of beauty; like Thoreau, I am eager to report the glory of the universe. Such is my belief and such is my legacy.

the End
.. Still beautiful ..